THE WAILING OF THE CHRIST-CHILD

A Book of Christmas Poems and Coloring Book

by

Mattie Shavers Johnson
Limited Edition, 1994

i

International Standard Book Number: 1-886663-03-3

The cover speaks to the belief that Christ is the only Son of God, born and offered for sacrifice because of God's love for humankind.

Through Jesus Christ, the Anointed One, the Messiah, the Savior, we are atoned. He pleads for forgiveness of our sins by constantly wailing or pleading through his teachings.

As we pray and listen to His voice by honoring His birth, we receive His gift of eternal life.

He calls from the foothills of Arkansas ... or the hill tops of the Carolinas ... or the valley of the Dakotas ... or beside the sea ... or over the rocky land and pebbles ... or in the sand dunes of Africa. He calls — constantly and tenderly — "Follow Me."

PRINTED IN THE UNITED STATES OF AMERICA

CHATMAN PRESS
P. O. Box 121121
Nashville, TN 37212

God's Gifts

of Love.

His Birth

and

Sacrifice

To my Family

and

All Children

at Heart.

ACKNOWLEDGMENTS

To Dr. Vera S. Chatman, my deepest appreciation for her gracious support and kind consideration as publisher. To Mrs. Norma White, I extend my sincere appreciation for her time and evaluation; to Ms. Audrey D. Hall, my hardy thanks for being supportive and helpful in the production of this book of poems; to Mrs. M. O. Collins for her suggestions and love; to Mrs. J. V. Benton for expressing encouragement and a need for her students to have this kind of experience; to Col. I. E. Shavers for his encouragement and love; to Mrs. Emma Wisdom for bringing out the "writer" in me; to Dr. Richard Carter and staff for use of an office; to my family for indulging me in my special interest and love. Without all of these kinds of support, this book would have never been completed.

Much of the inspiration for writing this book of poems is credited to reading portions of the Holy Bible. The King James Version: Matthew, Mark, Luke and John.

ABOUT THE AUTHOR

Mattie Shavers Johnson is an accomplished educator, lecturer, author, poet and musician. She has taught at the elementary through college levels, written and performed both piano compositions and poetry in a variety of settings and on many occasions.

She has produced a community guide book and published several chap books. Her early public speaking earned honors in high school and college.

Johnson is a native of Garland Community, DeKalb, Texas, the eighth child (a twin) of four brothers and six sisters born to Robert S. Shavers and Laura Garland Shavers.

She earned a Bachelor of Science degree from Tennessee State University at Nashville, Tennessee, Master of Science from Hunter College at New York City and Master of Science in Public Health from Meharry Medical College at Nashville. As a concerned educator, Johnson established a scholarship in the name of her parents at Fisk University also in Nashville. Her Alma Mater, Meharry Medical College honored Johnson with a scholarship in her name for her many contributions to the institution. She has also given valuable service as a Girl Scout board member, and a choir director of music.

Johnson is a member of St. Andrews Presbyterian Church.

After thirty successful years in the teaching profession, she devotes her time exclusively to her writing and volunteer work.

Johnson is married to Dr. C. W. Johnson, Vice President Emeritus of Meharry Medical College. The Johnsons have spent most of their adult life in Nashville. Their three children are now adults.

ABOUT THE BOOK

Mattie Shavers Johnson, author of Wings of Fire: Desert Storm, Desert Shield and Desert Calm, which has been very well received, now brings to the public a Collection of Christmas Poems for Children, Youth and Adults: "The Wailing of the Christ-Child."

The book of Christmas poems with a coloring book is about the meaning of Christmas: The birth of Christ and the significance of God's gift of love. It is also about the constant pleading through Jesus Christ for all of us to be aware of our transgressions toward others. His love for mankind and the forgiveness of our sins. It adds the feature of entertaining Children by including a coloring book to help them understand the meaning of Christmas and His (God's) love.

Johnson's works have appeared in Journals, Newsletters and newspapers anthologies Chap Books and newspapers. And she has personally done numerous readings to a wide audience in universities, bookstores, schools and organizations.

The Wailing of the Christ-Child is divided into three parts:

Part I: Poems for Children And A
Coloring Book: What Santa Means to Me

Part II: Poems for Youth and Adults:
"The Christ-Child: Blessed Is He"

Part III: The Wailing of the Christ-Child
For Adults and the Young at Heart and Other Poems

TABLE OF CONTENTS

DEDICATION iii
ACKNOWLEDGEMENT iv
ABOUT THE AUTHOR v
ABOUT THE BOOK vi
TABLE OF CONTENTS vii
POETIC STATEMENT xi

PART I: POEMS FOR CHILDREN AND A COLORING BOOK:
WHAT SANTA MEANS TO ME

Color Me Christmas 1
Color Me Joy 2
Dance With Me 3
Color Me the Faces of Children 4
Color Me Patience 5
It's Christmas Time 6
Color Me Hope 7
Color Me Joy 8
Color Me Peace 9
Color Me Freedom 10
Color Me a Secret Place 11
Hide 'n Seek 12
Color Me in a Manger 13
Color Me a Light Through a Window 14
God's Glory 15
What the Christ Child Will Accept 16
Color Me a Message 17

Table of Contents Cont'd

Beat the Drum 18

Color Me the Answer 19

Color Me Wise 20

The Baby Awakes 21

Color Me a Gift of Love 22

Santa — His Bag and Boots 23

Color Me Happy 24

What I Want for Christmas 25

My Gift 26

Color Me A Mystery 27

The Christ Child 28

Children Can't Wait 29

Color Me a Snow Flake 30

White Christmas 31

Color Me Love 32

King of Love 33

Color Me a Tree of Life 34

My Christmas 35

Color Me a Cross 37

Color Me Bread of Life 38

Color Me Faith 39

Color Me a Pure Heart for Service 40

Color Me Life 41

Color Me Faith 42

Color Me a Beautiful Day 43

Table of Contents Cont'd

PART II: POEMS FOR YOUTH AND ADULTS
THE CHRIST: BLESSED IS HE

A Savior Is Born 45

After the Chaff Has Blown .46

In Quest of an Inner Voice .47

The Beatitudes 48

Who Is Santa Claus 49

He's Coming 51

The Miracle 52

The Last Crust of Bread 53

His Voice 54

Two Rivers 55

His Birth 56

What Have I to Give Him 57

Joys of Christmas 59

The Hood 61

A Sign of the Times 63

Faith, Hope, and Love 65

The Night Grows Brighter .66

To Keep His Love Ev'er Blooming 67

The Future of Our Years 68

A Note to the Christ Child .69

PART III: WAILING OF THE CHRIST-CHILD
FOR ADULTS AND THE YOUNG AT HEART — AND OTHER POEMS

Wailing of the Christ-Child 71

Christ 72

New Born Wonderment 73

Table of Contents Cont'd

A Biblical Statement 74

The Wise Men 75

Not Just for Christmas 77

The Coming 78

No Room in the Inn 79

Little White Snowflake 80

What I Like 81

Come Feed My Sheep 83

Come to Me 84

Epiphany 85

Be Not Alarmed 86

The Little Stranger 87

Love One Another 88

At Dawning 89

His Mother's Love 90

He Is Love 92

The Palm 93

Faith 94

Marching to the Beat 95

Essence of the Force 96

Winter's Hope 97

Till He Comes Again 98

The Faces of God's Children 100

Haiti 101

Hope and Love With All Seasons 102

Peace on Earth 103

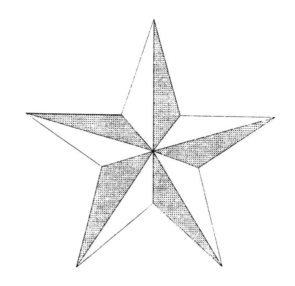

A star was born
one wintry night
Beside a sea enthralled
Illuminating God's delight,
A captive of man's soul.

MSJ
From: "Sharing," 1976
To: Phillip N. and Sheila

PART I: CHRISTMAS POEMS FOR CHILDREN AND A COLORING BOOK: WHAT SANTA MEANS TO ME

COLOR ME JOY

DANCE WITH ME

COLOR ME THE FACES OF CHILDREN

COLOR ME PATIENCE

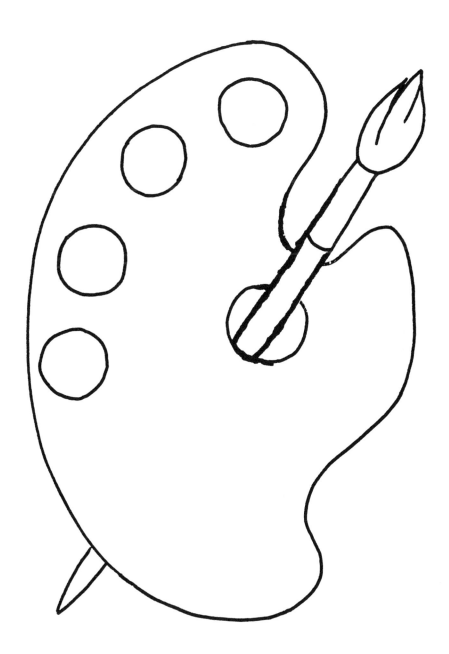

IT'S CHRISTMAS TIME

It's Christmas time!
It's Christmas time!
See the tinsel on the tree?
It's Christmas time!
It's Christmas time!
The snowflakes are falling.
Come dance with me!
Come dance with me!

Santa is Coming!
Santa is Coming!
Wonder what he's bringing me?
Dog and sleigh?
A doll maybe.
Let us play
"Ring around the roses"
"A pocket full of posies"

Santa is Coming!
Santa is Coming!

To: Livette

COLOR ME HOPE

THE LITTLE PRINCE

Children love him
everywhere.
They go to His House
to play and pray.
They sing with the choir
of angels there
And listen to what
He has to say.

TO: Phillip M.

COLOR ME JOY

COLOR ME PEACE

BIBLICAL STATEMENT

Suffer the little children to come unto me, and forbid them not; for of such is the Kingdom of God.

St. Mark 10:14

To: Joi and Jamie

COLOR ME FREEDOM

I LOVE BABY JESUS

I love the Baby Jesus
He always smiles at me
Even when I'm sad
He gives me joy on Christmas
morn,
And forgets when I've
been bad.

To: Glen, Shelisa and Chad

COLOR ME A SECRET

HIDE 'N SEEK

Come on in children!
Gather around.
This is Baby Jesus.
You can teach Him
Games of this town.

He will teach you
His games of 'Lost and Found.'

Hide 'n Seek is His favorite
game.
He knows secret places
You've been. He shoulders all blame.
You can go behind the
Great Divide.
You can run. He is your place to hide.

TO: Wendy and Avon

COLOR ME IN A MANGER

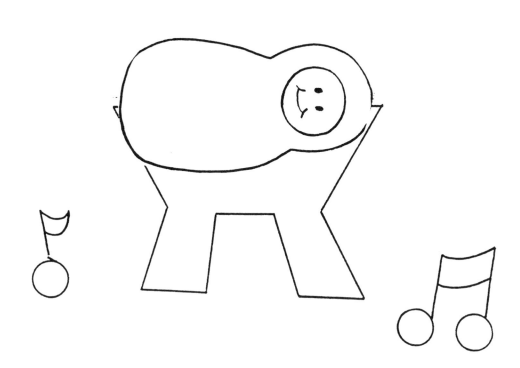

COLOR ME A LIGHT THROUGH A WINDOW

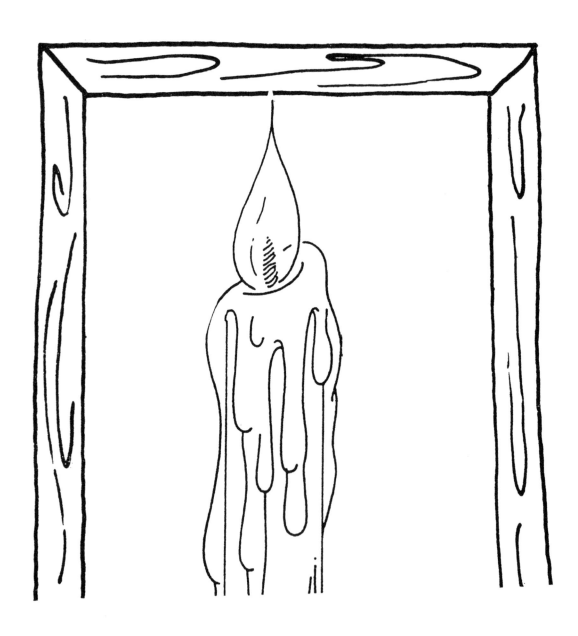

COLOR ME HOPE

GOD'S GLORY

His glory shines
Through the window
of Christ,
That we may be
redeemed.
His birth tells a
beautiful story
Of our sins and transgressions
washed clean.

TO: Skip - C.W., Jr.

15

WHAT THE CHRIST-CHILD WILL ACCEPT

The Christ-Child
will accept
Your worn out and bent-
up toys.
Of greed, hate and
malice.
He makes them new
again,
With polish of
forgiveness,
And wipes away
all pain.
Fall on your knees!
Bow to the father!
Ask for His blessings too.
He will cleanse your weary years
through the Christ,
And wipe your tears from the chalice of sorrows.
He will watch over you.
His message is: "Start Anew!"

TO: Robert

COLOR ME A MESSAGE

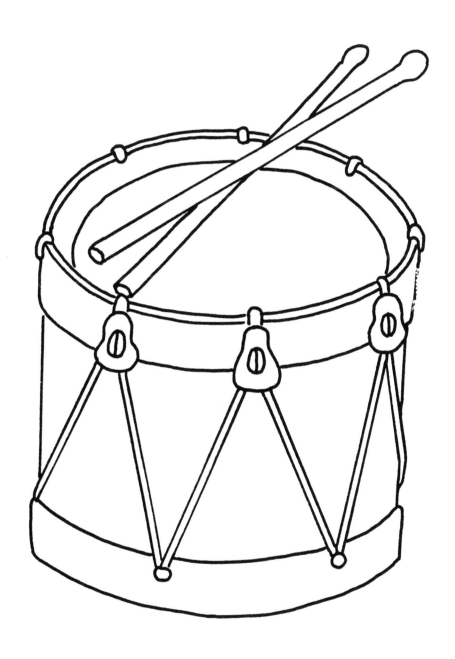

BEAT THE DRUMS

Beat the drum to carry
the message.
Let it resound on
every hill;
A Savior comes,
as it was written.
Let the angels proclaim,
"It has been fulfilled!"

TO: Lorenzo and Jean's Children

COLOR ME THE ANSWER

COLOR ME WISE

THE BABY AWAKES

The stars watched
Baby Jesus
As He lay sleeping
in the manger.
The cattle were
lowing,
at break of day.
The baby awakes.
He smiles and plays.

Mother washes baby
in frankincense
And smoothes his
swaddling clothes,
Then gently places
Him in the hay
To watch the sheep
silently.

TO: Mildred and Garfield's Children

COLOR ME A GIFT OF LOVE

SANTA - HIS BAG AND BOOTS

Down the chimney
All covered with soot
Came Santa with bag,
His treasures, red suit and black boots.

He almost sneezed.
That would have blown his disguise.
So, he covered his mouth,
But read all notes twice.

He filled all stockings,
Left by the fire,
Then said a short prayer
As he raised his red cap high.

He drank his milk, ate his cookies,
And with a ho, ho, ho,
Called Blitzen, Donner, Dancer, Dasher
Cupid, Prancer Comet and Vixen, his
rookies.
Then quickly closed the darkened door.

Off he went
Through the midnight air
The children were still asleep;
Awaiting the bright morning glare,
To see their toys and a Merry
Christmas, everywhere!

TO: Myrtle and Bernard's Children

23

COLOR ME HAPPY

WHAT I WANT FOR CHRISTMAS

I want a doll for
Christmas.
I'll dress her in the
finest threads.
I'll sing a lullaby to
her,
And tuck her safely
in bed.

I want a little whistle.
I lost mine yesterday.
I want to call my dog, Thistle
When he's lost, and can't find his way.

TO: Millie and Alvin's Children

25

MY GIFT

I did not bring Him
silver or gold.
When I followed the
star to the East
I had no means for
frankincense or myrrh
often sold.
To Kings from the Orient
Who wear them to fancy feasts.

The only gift I gave to Him
While lying in the manger
Was a lullaby. I sang
to Him

For to me, He was
no stranger.

TO: Helen and Ennis' Children

COLOR ME A MYSTERY

THE CHRIST CHILD

He's coming by air.
No, He's coming by plane.
Maybe by elephant.
Oh, I think a train.

Who's going to greet Him?
What is His name?
I'll call Him the Christ-child
Any name is the same.

TO: Jim and Lorraine's Children

CHILDREN CAN'T WAIT

Hear the patter
of little feet
Coming down
the hallway!
Santa has left
a special treat
For expectant hands
To reach out and keep.

Much too early
For a bike in-house,
But Children Can't Wait.
Even after given advice
Which ones they can play with,
Quiet and nice;
Before the break
of dawn.

TO: Lorenzo and Clarice's Children

29

WHITE CHRISTMAS

Look at those snow flakes
coming down!
We're going to have a
white Christmas!
Now we can see Santa's footprints
on the ground.
We will know when
He's come around.

Look at the stars shining
through the clouds!
What does it mean? Its a
mystery of our Lord.
Its a miracle!

He sends us snowflakes
and the morning star.

TO: Fred and Willis' Children

COLOR ME A SNOWFLAKE

COLOR ME LOVE

KING OF LOVE

In a city
Called Bethlehem
Where Jesus Christ
was born
Joseph and Mary;
His parents
Gave thanks unto
the Lord,
For a Son they
gave back to Him.
Sent down from
heaven above.
With love and peace
in His heart
He could be
Non'other
Than the Prince
of peace
Sent by God.
He is our
Precious Savior
A gift we treasure,
all,
A King in all
His glory
A shining light
from above
He is the King of love.

TO: Jenna and Bent

33

MY CHRISTMAS

I was sleeping
under a tree.
Then I was dreaming
with plenty company.

A little top.
I spent it around;
A beautiful doll
All dressed and gowned.

Christmas carols
In the background.
Toys to ride,
that glide
Cars and pride.

Kitchen stoves,
Clowns to giggle,
Jungle Jims and doves
And things that wiggle.

Nutcrackers and candy;
A China Cabinet.
Bubble gum and "Bandy"
But none left out to fret.

COLOR ME A TREE OF LIFE

Many hugs and kisses:
No hits and misses.
All the world's, children
smiled at me.
That was my Christmas.

TO: Honey and Pauline's Children

36

COLOR ME A CROSS

COLOR ME BREAD OF LIFE

COLOR ME FAITH

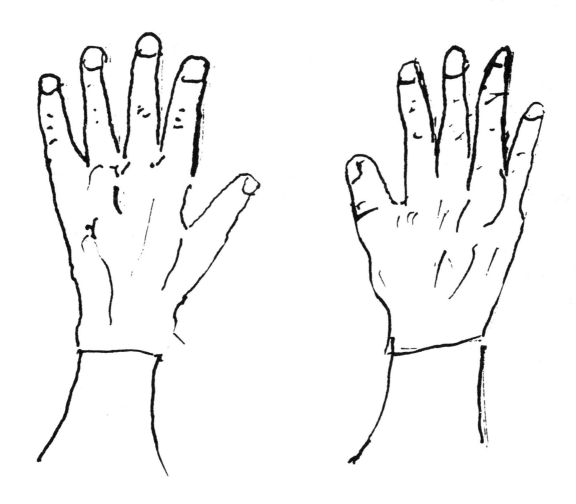

COLOR ME A PURE HEART FOR SERVICE

COLOR ME LIFE

COLOR ME FAITH

COLOR ME A BEAUTIFUL DAY

PART II: POEMS FOR YOUTH AND ADULTS
THE CHRIST: BLESSED IS HE

A SAVIOR WAS BORN

And so, it came to pass
On that bright morning,
A Savior was born
At the break of dawning.
A cross He must carry
for all who sin,
In a sinful world
Though born as King.

May His innocence of
That bright dazzling night
Be as free as a flying
dove;
Its quill dipped in love
To overcome our silent grief;
In conquest of that mighty love,
Victory, after disbelief.

TO: Andrea, Cheryl and Deryl

IN QUEST OF AN INNER VOICE

A journey in quest of
an inner voice,
A mystery, and the burden
of choice.
Gifts to barter, forgiveness
of sin
Pleading of a Child to let
Him come in.

AFTER THE CHAFF HAS BLOWN

There is no need to thrash
the wheat
After the Chaff has
blown.
The soul is purified after
suffering defeat,
As Christ in the manger
has shown.

THE BEATITUDES

Blessed are the poor in spirit; for their's is the
    kingdom of heaven.
Blessed are they that mourn; for they shall
    be comforted.
Blessed are the meek; for they shall inherit
    the earth.
Blessed are they which do hunger and thirst after
    righteousness; for they shall be filled.
Blessed are the merciful; for they shall
    obtain mercy.
Blessed are the pure in heart; for they shall
    see God.
Blessed are the peacemakers; for they shall be
    called the children of God.
Blessed are they which are persecuted for righteousness
    sake for theirs is the kingdom of heaven.
Blessed are we when men shall revile you, and
    persecute you, and shall say all manner of
    evil against you falsely, for my sake.
Rejoice, and be exceedingly glad; for great is your
    reward in heaven; for persecuted they
    the prophets which were before you.

Matthew 5:3-12

WHO IS SANTA CLAUS?

Who is Santa Claus to you?
Dancer, Prancer, and rest of crew?
Tinsel, red tassel and bright blue?
Who is Santa Clause to you?

Fairies leaping in the air?
Snow-flakes twinkling everywhere?
Amethyst foil on door with care?
Anticipated gifts, not there?

Trees of silver, colors all bright?
Mistletoe to wish on, no frost-bite?
Endless chains of decoration, just right?
Waiting for that snowy night!?

Hidden dreams to bring forth at day break?
To adorn the emotions and for yuletide sake?
Spinning photographic yarns, baking a cake?
Unknown Spirits, we should not partake?

Bearded looks and suites of red?
On each corner, Oh! E-gad!
Dragging children on arms of lead
Through the streets and stores-weird?

Passing strangers loaded with cares?
Eyes beyond, but casting blank stares?
Hoping they've seen your dress and wares
But not question your affairs?

Suppose we all had Santa Suits
Inside and out a-blaze with fruits
of kindness in our heart, from roots
Entwine, stepping in each others boots?

The question would now be answered true
In voice, in deed, in blessings too,
A gift; The Giver, bells ringing a-new
Who Santa is, is me to you.

HE'S COMING

Today, I will feed the
cattle well
And leave them plenty
hay.
I read the heavens very
well.
He's coming to the stables
to stay.

These humble gifts I give
to Him
Tho not for a King's
abode,
Will serve to deceive while
Angels watch over Him
And while music spears the
slumber cloud.

I'll welcome Him rest
from His journey
A welcome hay-mat to greet
Him best.
Tho shamed am I, not worthy.
A chance to receive Him gladly
For I am his servant, deemed
sinner each day.

THE MIRACLE

A candle in every window
Hope in each creatures heart
A burning dream for tomorrow;
a plan for another start.

The wonder of creation,
The miracle of birth a-new,
The beauty of coronation
The gentleness of the ewe.

The star that shines above us
To lead us to a Savior;
The songs of gladness and trust
of a God to see us through.

THE LAST CRUST OF BREAD

O, Sweet Baby Jesus, please tell my Lord
We are still hungry
down in Africa.
We still fight over
the last crust of bread.
And many are dying
or found dead
Floating down the
Nile.

HIS VOICE

His voice is heard when
the morning breaks;
When breezes blow and
the birds sing;
When prayers are said
and bread we take;
When children are playing;
When church choirs are singing
When rain is falling
and flowers spring.

TWO RIVERS

There is a river
Called Euphrates.
There is a river
Called Tigris.
The two rivers meet
at civilization's feet
Where Summer begins
on the Potter's knees.

HIS BIRTH

It's all about love
and sacrifice;
Forgiveness of a
friend;
Fellowship, and trust
of your fellowman;
And love of God.
Even after you've
sinned.

WHAT HAVE I TO GIVE HIM?

What have I to give Him?
The chairs have lost
all their legs.
The table is falling
down.
The stove only burns
wood-pegs.
I get water from
the ground.

What have I to give Him?
My horse has
gone lame.
The wagon has lost
its last wheel.
The cupboard is bare
of game.
I have no bread
to give.

What have I to give Him?
My clothes are tattered
and torn.
My feet are bare to
the bone.
I have broken my
last hoe.
Nothing to grow.

What have I to give Him?
I talked to everyone

I could meet.
They say, "don't give up
in defeat;
Give Him your talents
one by one.
Give Him you sweet
smile.
Throw away your
gun.
Work to feed another
child.

Bring your tithes to
give in the plate.
Say your prayers
before its too late.
Watch the trees and
flowers grow.
Give Him your love
and watch it soar.

JOYS OF CHRISTMAS

Sing the Yuletide joys
of Christmas
In whose honor shall
it be?
Tradition dictates before
the feast
Who ultimately tops
the highest tree.

He is the guest
of honor.
This is His table
today.
The chalice is raised;
we break the bread
Of forgiveness, and
quietly pray.

Deck the halls,
Clean and open
the house
Pick the finest
nuts
Make ready for
the coming. Rejoice.

Bake white cakes.
cookies and cupcakes.
Put delicious pies
in the oven.

The turkey is
all baked
The vegetables
crisply done.

Set the finest table.
Pour the favorite
wine.
Napkins to match
when able.
Now, flat-ware
the Best kind.

Bow all lowly heads.
For everyone to
give thanks.
After the blessing
and all are fed
Depart, with your
family rank.

THE HOOD

My Mama don't know
when she's working,
Mostly when she could,
I'm shooting up, cracking up,
and drinking up.
In the neighborhood.

The brothers and sisters
come by my pad
With bags and boom boom
boxes
And I feel like I'm king
Singing and laughing. Man I'm bad!

I put on my finest
threads,
To get my bread.
My Mama don't know
I'm stealing,
And I haven't seen my dad.

There are guns everywhere.
My finger is hot.
I'm never satisfied
with what I've got.
The police are watching daily.
They only need a body bag
and shots.

I am wild and foolish
I have no conscious
yet.
If I live to be twenty years old,
I've already lost my soul.
Don't cry Mama and Daddy
I'm just trying to be
Somebody rich and
special,
Or just "somebody," - somebody!
Please!
Help me!

A SIGN OF THE TIMES

There was once a brilliant star
Predicting and guiding us to where we are.
You cannot tell me its a
sign of the times
When black men are falling
like flies
From failure of friends;
guilt denied.

Mothers are weeping
For children who've died,
But Gabriel's horn
Has not been blown.

Resources are short,
But everyone can be sold
or brought.
AIDS is rampant.
Cancer fought.

No place to hide.
Many hoops to jump.

Rwanda is waining.
The people defying; and complaining.
All caught up
In their own trespassing.
And yet you tell me.
Its a sign of the times?

Rwanda is turning its people
to stone,
Strewn across the land
Facing the sun.

Maybe this is a sign
Of a fatalistic mind
Consuming itself;
Defying its time
to give birth,
Or wish for death.

When we reach the
impossibility of reason
Every man is out
of season,
And there are no
Fulfillments brought
to bare.

FAITH, HOPE AND LOVE

Faith, hope and love abide
In Chambers of sullen draped
longing.
Faith to swallow a boasting pride.
Hope to diminish love's
sorrowing.

THE NIGHT GROWS BRIGHTER

The night grows brighter with
each star born
To lighten the way for each crown
worn of thorn.
The day only comes to pay
homage in turn,
For each blessing encountered,
or each flower shown.

TO KEEP HIS LOVE EV'ER BLOOMING

Heavenly Sky,
Why do you pour down
Your moonlight and stars
upon the earth
To kiss the manger
Before day births?

To keep His love ev'er
blooming?
"Without His light,
Love would surely
die,
Before the sun breaks,
All creatures would
defy
His Coming."

THE FUTURE OF OUR YEARS

Here lies the future of our years
All mapped out in hope and thought;
Bound by perplexity and silent tears
Facing the stars the Christ-Child wrought.

The glowing heavens light our way
Along endless paths of forests-dark;
A little child to love, honor and obey;
With trust and a song of the Lark.

Behold, our hearts, our mansions wide,
Stretched forth with gifts we share,
Absent of self and all our pride
We lay at the altar with care.

Wise men at pastorial gates await
On landscapes with flocks by night,
To see the miracle and man relate
To harmonious beauty and God's might.

All is quiet. Still's the night.
Baby soon will awake,
To announce the dawning of new light
With voice rising high as the sun breaks.

A NOTE TO THE CHRIST CHILD

Dear Jesus,
Your children are still
Wandering in the streets
Killing each other
And drinking the swill.

No wonder, for they
have no ears,
And have closed their eyes
to all their fears;
Of mankind's wrath against
themselves; their peers.
O, when will the
morning come?
When will there be
peace?
Your wailing not heard
has ceased.
Or is it I who flunked
the test?
Did I not heed the
infants request?

PART III: WAILING OF THE CHRIST CHILD: FOR ADULTS AND THE YOUNG AT HEART AND OTHER POEMS

WAILING OF THE CHRIST CHILD

Hear the wailing of the Christ-Child:
No hospitality or justice for those
Who have no home nor reconcile.
Just hunger or illness; only those man chose

Who hears the wailing of **inhumanity;**
The reality of the hearts of men;
No room to grow and blossom gladly;
The gifts the Giver proclaims over
and over again?

The Mother hears and often comforts
Those hearts riveted and left to sin;
Heard only by her through His Son
Who hears and answers the needs of men.

She feels the tugging on her body
To feed lost souls and comfort, when,
No one will answer and the mighty
And ruthless exclaim: No room
in the Inn!!

CHRIST

"The coming of a Christ (Messiah) was foretold often in the Old Testament, perhaps the most notable prophesy being in Isaiah 9:11. He was to be of the House of David; justice and righteousness never ending would be established on His coming. This was not universally accepted; there were many unbelievers when Jesus was born, who remained unbelievers throughout His life. The believers accepted Him as God the Son, the second members of the Trinity, Christ (meaning the anointed one) the Messiah, the one foretold: Jesus the Christ, Christ Jesus. His complete acceptance of Himself as the Son of God had its influence in winning many doubters, and the incomparable beauty and power of His preaching influence constantly increasing numbers of mankind."

From: Dictionary of the Bible
King James Version

NEW BORN WONDERMENT

A contest rages in the
elements;
A drama begins to
form.
A curtain is raising
the audience's alarm;
Captives of new-born
Wonderment.

A BIBLICAL STATEMENT

"For God so loved the
world, that he gave his
only begotten Son, that
Whosoever believeth in
Him should not perish
but have everlasting life."

John 3:16

WISE MEN

(Three Kings)

The Camel's backs were laden
with Myrrh
Frank incense was abundant
too
They traveled along the Red Sea Bank
To Egypt, Babylon and then Syria.
There were gifts to treasure.
The Wise Men knew,
And they wanted to share them with
official rank.

The stars shone brighter than mid day
sun
Far to the East. They wondered.
Could this be the Master's promise?
A magnet drew them farther beyond
And over the dunes. In their hearts
they pondered,
Knowing the answer, for they were
wise.

They reached the manger and wept
joyously,
Unburdening their hearts in Oriental gifts.
Then left after warning the host, of
danger.
Into the night they sped, and hid
constantly.
But leading the watchers

astray, as if
They were following a
caravan
But away from the manger.

NOT JUST FOR CHRISTMAS

Not just for Christmas
But for everyday.
Let Him come into your hearts
With the spirit of giving
That we may receive,
A blessing conceived in love.

Sing praises to the
Christ Child.
Comfort His every need
Bring Him succor
from your heart
He thrives from
others you feed.

THE COMING

Stars lying to the East
of five gates
Seek togetherness as fingers
to hand;
Their secrets hide beyond
fateful man
Before the fire of approaching
dawn.

Let the earth observe
their journey
Let the people sing their
blessings,
For the light has come
in winter
And no shadows diminish
the warning.

NO ROOM IN THE INN

Mothers are always on the
donkey's back
Going some place to birth
a truth,
Most times alone, to bare
her pain
With no room in the
Inn.

Only she can know
When secret sorrows come.
For she dries her bitter tears
On His precious garments.

LITTLE WHITE SNOWFLAKE

Little white snowflake
From the heavenly sky,
What is your message?
Why must you die?

Your crystalline body
Floats swiftly to the ground
N'er looking back,
As the dawning becomes the dawn.

"I cover the seedlings on the ground;
I cover the feet of flowers not born;
I cover the bloom of each blushing rose;
Indeed, I'd die with a crown and thorn."

"My blanket is warm
For I lay at the knees
Of leaves that weep when winter turns ,
My breath is sweet on the sunlet burn."

"I drift down mountains
and wash the plains,
From shore to shore in persiflage.
And sometimes mingle with the rain."

"My journey is ne'er absent of pain
But I give birth to the seasons, over and over again."

WHAT I LIKE

I like my dolls
before Christmas.
I like my turkey
and my clowns.
I like food
always baking.
In fact, I like Christmas
All year round.
I like candy bars
in November.
My frost on pumpkins
in May;

Sporty cars
and bicycle bars,
All ready to play
with each day.

I like fancy clothes,
housing and browsing.
More fancy cars;
I'll take two bran new.
My drinks strong too,
Give me one, No two.

I like friendships
without relations;
Loving without
passion or partaking;
Friends I don't
pursue.
If this is my cake,
I'll eat it too.

COME FEED MY SHEEP

Touch one flower and
the world is your kin.
Breathe its fragrance
and its meaning transcends
Your soul and its reliance.

It is He. The Christ-Child
"Believe, He said, in me."
I am the way, the truth and light
Come feed my sheep for Thee.

COME TO ME

Come to me
Oh Lord, my Savior,
Come to me
Oh Lord, alone,
Speak to me.
In tongues of understanding
That I may see the light of mystery.
Lead me safely on.

EPIPHANY

The sun rose only
a few seconds earlier
To greet its swing in
all our favor.
A gift and promise
after winter
Free of spirits with
life to savor.

The December sun
slightly out of orbit,
Had set each day on
a programmed run,
But on this day, made
a sudden plummet.

The sun rose brighter;
another trial day
After the New Born Christ;
Steps and trackings with
the soltice.
But the beginnings
of Epiphany.

BE NOT ALARMED

Be not alarmed
About the Spirit of love;
All have touched
its sting.
None has more from
the Mother wing
For we brought it
with us
On morning's wonder.
We share its essence
Long after the song.
Its melody penetrates
all else
With the storm.
It lingers among
the wind and tide,
Centuries after we've
gone,
To join the Chorus
inside.

A LITTLE STRANGER

The sky gives promise
For a story you know well,
Told by the prophets
And angels, as they sing and tell.

It is enough for my heart to sing
When He came as a Savior;
A gift for others.
My gift, I bring.

Covers from gifts
Have been ripped away.
The people have gone,
All parted; some a-stray.

I am only a little stranger
Wrapped in swaddling clothes
Laying in a manger.
Come receive a message and hear my woes.

My heart pangs;
Clear as a tinkling bell.
I know I'm not worthy alone,
I have received the first-born.

LOVE ONE ANOTHER

Lord, you have shown us the
meaning of love,
By giving us the Christ-Child,
your Son;
A mystery all behold, yet know
That we can love others,
If we bow before you.

AT DAWNING

At dawning
What is duty bound?
The sun comes up
New options found.
A table set
All creatures sound
a message
in their song.

HIS MOTHER'S LOVE

A mother is a gift
from God.
Only children know
her name.
They call it each
or every morning
And the answer is
still the same.

She kisses them at
bedside,
And bids them to
act polite.
They say their prayers
in morning
And to bed before
the night.

A mother is a gift
from God.
How precious the
memory is;
Before the sun
is rising
I see her duties
fill.

Stronger than the
heavens above
Her love will last
eternal,
Blessing each, her
Children,
She sides with
everyone.

A Mother is a
precious gift
Cherish each moment
drifting,
Only a glimpse into
her life
But you've seen
centuries awakening.

HE IS LOVE

Trying to grow and see
the flowers bloom
Remind me each day that
love needs nurturing.
For the feelings that
one has,
And the beauty that
one sees,
Are only for the
taking.
The reaching out;
The touching of
one flower
and claiming it
for your own;
Nourishing this flower
that God has given
us all,
Is the spirit of love,
For He is love, and
We are His Children.

THE PALM

Take the palm and
walk to victory.
A choice not given
to thieves;
Swept away by waves
of iniquity
In waters unphantomed
when they dare to breathe.

Each day we're given
A cross and choices;
Palms to spread and
Victories to gain.
Each frond stripped
brings ringing voices,
As we leave bare
The Giver disdained.

FAITH

Faith is diversified;
Exciting to know;
Not confined to one way
of believing
But an existential reaching
out for some flow
Of redemption after
we've sinned.
Although not permanent,
It requires
Constant confessing.

All roads lead to
An ocean front;
Their name's no barring
Account.
Humanity's outlook is
the only fount;
A longing to make peace
With self and man
And leap from the
Abyss of destruction.

MARCHING TO THE BEAT

I have boycotted
When my children
Suffered, and felt defeat
and were in need.

I have walked the street
With my heart hanging
And hope in my feet.

Marching to the beat
of every song
And in days bygone,
To overcome grief.

I have cried
In the midst
Of stormy disbelief,
But kept on walking.

ESSENCE OF A FORCE

Asleep in each cocoon
we bear
The essence of a force,
and there,
In planned grace
We seek
A fortune left; our bread
We take.

Each day before the
sun we make
Another try at the door,
As we strive to open it
once more
To take our ordered
place for flight.

WINTER'S HOPE

Winter's stalk is cold and bare
With remnant artwork; slips of hair.
Nature's stomp of ardent frost
And chilly winds that welcome
lost.

The lacy meadows are still
with fright,
With the grip of winter's delight.
While sunlight peeks and shadows
fade,
As dancing dolls in Ice Capade.

Beware my friend, and be not
fain,
When caught in the vice
of old winter's reign.
Be quick to thank and
pay your borrow,
But most is seen in your
Mays tomorrow.

TILL HE COMES AGAIN

My soul was headed
toward the East
Where-in my faith and body
lie.
If it should stray without
thy peace
Where-to shall it demise?

My soul was headed toward
the West
My heart, my dimming light, my
peace abides.
It seeks to rest in idleness
But bids eternal love
to rise.

My soul was headed toward
the North
My body there would dare
not measure
Or enter the vault or
rustle forth
One moment of life's pleasure.

My soul was headed toward
the South
A warmer place to rest and seek.

Without a compass no
brevity in growth
Returns in anger its
seeking with grief.

My soul shall wander in a
troubled quest,
And seek Thy counsel once
more in pain.
The wrong endured from
sins of man
Shall reach for peace
as heavenness
Till He, (your Son) comes again

THE FACES OF GOD'S CHILDREN

The faces of God's children
In Rwanda's bloody war
Are as stormy sunsets
Against winters ironclad door.

No chance to come in
from the cold
When caught standing outside.
Society holds the last key
To frozen locks of pride.

Eyes look on quietly
Just watching blithely;
The swelling gorge politely
Consuming the deadly tide.

HAITI

A nation was born
Fleeing from oppression;
Black brothers and sisters
Stolen by aggression.

Beaten by other nations,
Chained to the rock,
Enslaved by a force,
More powerful than the "buck."

Rooted in the stench of sand
Grown to be a tree,
Nourished by loam sieved through,
The Ocean's belched-up debris.

Caught in tides of hatred company
They rise from the beveled ax
Severed and pruned, but fall constantly
For they feel the blade of destiny.

HOPE AND LOVE WITHIN ALL SEASONS

We all know the images
and joys of Christmas.
If we look with the eyes
of Children,
We will see and feel the
meaning of Christmas,
Knowing that hope and
love are lavished on
The universe
Within all its seasons.

PEACE ON EARTH

GOOD

WILL

TO MEN

A STRANGER COMES TODAY

Ding-a-ling, ling !
Ding-a-ling, ling!
Did you hear the door-bell ring?
"No, I didn't hear a thing."

Ding-a-ling, ling!
Ding-a-ling, ling!
It must be the cold wind blowing.
Look out the window pane
It's snowing! It's snowing!
And there are icicles on the weather vane.

Ding-a-ling, ling!
Ding-a-ling, ling!
Oh! I remember. Its Christmas!
A Stranger comes today.
We have no room. The sun rises soon.
I gave my word; He wants a home to stay.

Ding-a-ling-a-ling!
Ding-a-ling-a-ling!
Take Him to the barn
Then blow the loudest horn
Someone will come to take Him to the hay.

We are busy, and I have no time today.

Ding-a-ling-a-ling!
Ding-a-ling-a-ling!
Ding-a-ling-a-ling!
Ding-a-ling-a-ling!